CW01302179

LAMENTATIONS of the FLAME PRINCESS
ADVENTURES

NO REST FOR THE WICKED

BY
J. STUART PATE

ART
JEZ GORDON

LAYOUT AND CARTOGRAPHY
ALEX MAYO

COVER ART
YANNICK BOUCHARD

EDITING
JARRETT CRADER

Text © 2019 J. Stuart Pate
Issued Under Exclusive License

First Edition, First Printing 2019
Published by Lamentations of the Flame Princess
www.lotfp.com

Printed in Finland by Otava Book printing Ltd, Keuruu
ISBN 978-952-7238-24-0 (Print) / 978-952-7238-25-7 (PDF)

WAR IS HELL AND HELL IS OTHER PEOPLE

Central Europe is on fucking fire.

Despite the madness and supernatural horror of a typical campaign, characters must occasionally face the mundane world to add verisimilitude. Ideally this should be early and often, particularly since the activities of the average RPG session are often legally actionable. A group of well-armed mercenary-types, beholden to no kingdom and constantly venturing into well-guarded keeps and crypts, pulling riches out of the womb of the earth? In any sane world those are the exact sorts of people about whom you're going to have an opinion, no matter your station in life.

A contemporary example: imagine if a group of maniacs, outfitted like Blackwater mercenaries, came into your town robbing banks, digging up graves, and carefully infiltrating the sewer system. Even if they're particularly subtle and well-liked, important people are going to recognize that they came through, especially if they dropped several hundred thousand dollars on the local bars and left a couple of bastard children nine months later. Even ignoring the obvious legal ramifications, those sorts of people are constantly one step away from being branded as enemies of the state and that is assuming they're well-liked local heroes and not sociopaths: the innkeeper who just made a year's salary from one night of partying probably likes you well enough even if you caused some trouble, but the people whose ancestors were exhumed, the people whose reputations were ruined, and the unwed mothers left behind probably have a much less charitable opinion of the proceedings.

More importantly for a game billed as *Weird Fantasy Role-Playing* is that if every encounter or mystery includes the Weird, the supernatural bits cease to be Weird at all. To keep the Weird exotic it has to be juxtaposed with the mundanities of life. There's a world out there and it doesn't revolve around the characters or the Weird. The world continues if they do not. The characters are only special if they make themselves special.

And finally, central Europe is on fire. The conflicts currently rocking the area have been ongoing for fifteen years with no end in sight. Coupled with the witch hunts and the plagues it looks like the world is ending. That should constantly be simmering in the background, infecting your campaign, and threatening to boil over at any moment. It should lend a sense of urgency to play. The helpful NPC you just met could catch plague and be dead in a month. The village in which you're staying could be razed next week while you're away. The ancient evil you're trying to lock in that dungeon could be freed tomorrow by the soldiers seeking shelter for the night.

THE SETUP

The characters arrive at an inn between two other points of interest. Once they arrive, there is a timeline of events that will occur if they do not involve themselves, although they can intervene at any time. The question they have to answer is whether it's worth their time and effort to interfere, and are they willing to live with the consequences of their decisions? How do they feel about the families torn apart in the aftermath?

As written this adventure assumes a vague setting of eastern Bohemia in spring of 1632, but your players probably won't care unless they're experts on this stuff. Just drop the inn and the nearby army camp anywhere in your campaign, preferably between two points more than a day or so apart.

This probably isn't your first time adapting an adventure, so if you're setting it elsewhere or ignoring the early modern implied setting, you know what to do. Swap the Lutherans and Catholics if you're farther north, or switch the factions for any warring factions and oppressed minorities in your campaign.

Make note of the party's composition if you stick to early modern Earth. All player choices should mean something in a campaign, and if the characters don't match the local demographic, people are going to remember them. Magic-Users and Specialists may be questioned more intensely than other characters, the former for their potential blasphemies, the latter as potential spies. Also note that if anybody has a gonzo name — *"Oh, yeah, I'm Bob-hotep II"* — someone is going to ask about it.

SIDEBAR: TIMELINE IN BRIEF

- The characters arrive and meet the Herzogs and the Steiners.

- Griswold returns home and announces that soldiers are approaching.

- The Steiners hide in the cellar.

- Katharina Ruppel, Anna Engel, and their mercenaries arrive just after dusk.

- Katharina mentions they're looking for Imperial deserter Lodwig Steiner, the butcher of Wendisch Rindorf.

- Katharina and company will be the last to bed. They will report any suspicious activity to the army camp.

- Sergeant Johann Orth and a squad of ten soldiers arrive around 2 a.m. They will demand to search everyone.

- When the soldiers reach the cellar the Steiners open fire. The soldiers kill the family in the ensuing bloodbath.

BACKGROUND

Griswold Herzog was basically a kid when he went to fight for the Catholic League, and returned from the war a battle-scarred veteran. He saw enough atrocities to become disillusioned with the righteousness of the cause. While it wouldn't be accurate to say he lost his faith, he did lose his taste for the whole affair. He still believes in God, but maybe Man isn't the best shepherd of His teachings.

Returning from the front, he set about building his family a home in the foothills of the Ore Mountains, trying to stay remote enough to stay out of the war. The Herzog homestead was hardly remote enough, however, as people would still pass through the region. Griswold started trading with travelers, and over time his budding trading post required expansion. Over the past couple of years he has added to the trading post, building a full-fledged inn he calls *"The Soldier's Rest."* He and Jarla have added to the family since he returned home as well: Otto, Ilsa, and Gretchen have all been born within the past five years. The money earned by the inn and trading post manages to supplement their farming such that the Herzogs live very comfortably.

The main thing threatening their steading is the fact that Griswold has allowed Protestant Union espionage agents to use his inn as a dead drop location and meeting house. Jarla is aware of these activities although his children do not know. The dead drop is located at the old linden tree as listed on the map at the end of this book.

The Soldier's Rest is remote enough that this might not normally be a problem, but two days ago the Steiner family came to the inn seeking refuge. Part of Griswold's network of spies and ne'er-do-wells, the Steiners are fleeing Catholic League persecution and trying to make their way north to the Protestant front of the war. Under normal circumstances they could probably just slip away under the cover of night, but Lodwig Steiner is officially recognized as a deserter from the Imperial Army and is known to have burned the village of Wendisch Rindorf to cover his escape. Agents of the Imperial Army would be very interested in his location and making an example out of him.

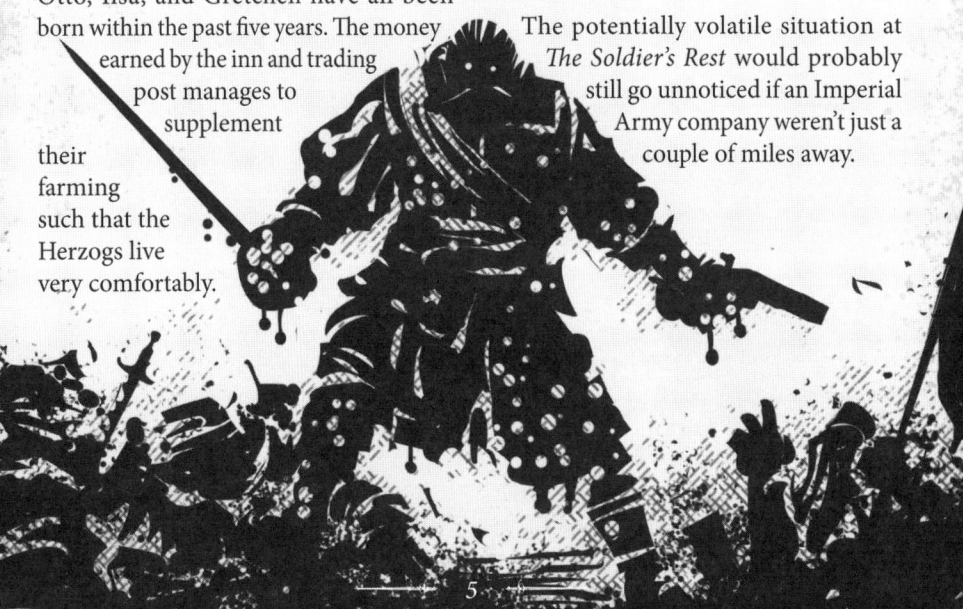

The potentially volatile situation at *The Soldier's Rest* would probably still go unnoticed if an Imperial Army company weren't just a couple of miles away.

TIMELINE

Yesterday Lodwig Steiner and his family arrived at *The Soldier's Rest*. Lodwig is a previous contact of Griswold and they trade information. Lodwig also knows Wallenstein's army is heading north, and fearing the potential for a meeting with Imperial soldiers, has requested sanctuary from the Herzogs for a couple of days until they can survey the area and definitively learn that they won't have any awkward encounters on the road.

Today the characters arrive around dusk, seeking to stay at the inn. If they arrive earlier in the day they find Gabriela tending bar and looking after the little ones as Griswold and Jarla perform various tasks around the farm. In the late afternoon Griswold goes riding to see if any sentries are coming.

When the characters arrive, Jarla is looking after baby Gretchen behind the bar while Gabriela helps serve. Griswold is absent. Otto and Ilsa are trying to occupy themselves, probably by eating with the Steiner children. Wilhelmina Steiner is feeding baby Alexa at the table near the fireplace while Lodwig and their children Waldemar, Konrad, and Dieter are eating at the table with her.

The following events occur thereafter:

- The Steiners are polite but don't expressly seek to speak with the characters. If asked they merely claim to be passing through, heading north to look for work and escape the fighting. Anyone watching them can see that their interactions are fairly loving; Lodwig helps young Dieter cut up his food and is showing him how to eat properly while Wilhelmina coos and fusses over baby Alexa.

- Jarla will offer any food or lodging requested. She will be sure to ask if the characters are refugees, hoping to gain some insight into their feelings about the war.

- Gabriela will try to learn anything she can about any far-off lands the characters may have experienced; as noted in her entry she's very interested in travelers.

- The characters will have a few minutes to talk or rest before Griswold Herzog returns to the inn. He stables his horse and dashes into the main room, informing the lot that soldiers are headed this way; he does not know if they will camp nearby or approach the inn but they may very well try to take anything of value for the war effort, so he understands if people want to find other lodgings for the night. The Steiners quietly pack their dishes and things and head back into the Herzogs' house rather abruptly. They have been hiding in the cellar and do not occupy any of the inn's rooms.

- Griswold and Jarla confer. Assuming Jarla's inquiries didn't find them to be particularly loyal to the military, Griswold will ask that the characters keep quiet about the Steiners if the soldiers arrive. The Steiners are Lutheran refugees, you see, and he suspects the soldiers will do something terrible if they are discovered. If the characters balk he is willing to offer them free lodging and up to 20sp per character to keep them quiet. He doesn't offer the money right away but if "free lodging" and "helping a family in need" don't motivate the characters, he'll start with 5sp or 10sp apiece before jumping to 20sp apiece. He'll pay them tomorrow when this is all over.

- Just after dusk Katharina Ruppel, Anna Engel, Jakob Deines, and Michael Kniess arrive at *The Soldier's Rest* and request rooms and stabling for their two horses. Pay close attention to anything the players say in their presence as they are Imperial spies. Presenting themselves as another band of travelers, Katharina will idly speak to the characters in an attempt to learn about them, although she will not probe overmuch. She may note that she saw a soldier's camp on the way here in an attempt to learn their feelings about the war, the Catholic League, and the Imperial Army.

- Katharina will also note that she heard the infamous outlaw Lodwig Steiner has been sighted in the area. He apparently deserted his post with the Imperial Army, and along with a few other soldiers stole supplies from his company and burned the village of Wendisch Rindorf to cover his escape. She doesn't know how many died in the fire or from the subsequent starvation over winter, but she's more interested in the 200sp reward for his capture. Intelligence suggests his family might have been in on it, too, so the Empire wants all of them.

- The intelligencers will get rooms, transfer their equipment to them, eat dinner, and play gambling games in the common room until the others go to sleep. If they learned anything suspicious about the characters or the inn Anna will go back to the army camp to report. Otherwise the travelers will eventually head to bed.

- If rooms are unavailable they will camp outside for the evening. If they cannot stable their horses they will hitch them either outside or near their camp.

- Whether they sleep inside or outside the inn, Katharina, Anna, Jakob, and Michael sleep in shifts: seven-and-a-half hours asleep, two-and-a-half hours on watch. Michael takes first watch followed by Jakob, Anna, and finally Katharina.

- Just before heading to bed Griswold will move one of the crates in the pantry over the trapdoor to the cellar, locking the Steiners in for the night.

- In the middle of the night, around 2 a.m. or so, Sergeant Johann Orth and a squad of ten soldiers enter the inn through the common room. They first loudly knock on the doors to the pantry and entryway and order anyone inside to open the doors. The noise from all the banging and shouting is likely to awaken everyone in the inn. Griswold Herzog will answer the door; Sergeant Orth will take five soldiers and search the Herzogs' quarters while the other five soldiers head upstairs and begin knocking on doors.

- When each occupant answers the soldiers will neatly explain that Protestant intelligence agents are suspected to be operating in this area. They have also received word that Lodwig Steiner, Imperial Army deserter and chief engineer of the razing of Wendisch Rindorf, is active in the area. There is a 200sp bounty for information leading to the capture or death of the Steiners as all are implicated in the slaughter of Wendisch Rindorf.

- They will then ask to search the room and the gear contained therein. If they are refused they will threaten force and a second refusal will likely result in a fight. Sounds of struggle will prompt the other five soldiers and Sergeant Orth to arrive as well.

- If a search yields any specialist's tools or spellbooks, they will call for Sergeant Orth. They assume specialist's tools are being used by espionage agents and will similarly assume spellbooks are encrypted missives. It is at the Referee's discretion whether any other items the characters carry suggest illegal activity. When Sergeant Orth arrives, he will question the characters; he will let them go if they can reasonably explain why they have these items. He's inclined to assume a heavily-armed party clearly built for traveling are mercenaries. Parties unable to explain any strange items will likely be escorted to the military camp for further interrogation.

- Assuming there are no interruptions, the five soldiers downstairs will investigate the house, the barn, and finally the pantry. They will discover the trapdoor while moving boxes and will head downstairs.

- Lodwig Steiner has heard the commotion and he and his family are huddled in the dark. When the door opens and he determines soldiers are coming downstairs, he and his wife open fire. One soldier goes down (although he can be revived), and when it is clear the two gunmen are reloading the rest of the soldiers pour down the stairs.

- The soldiers kill the family in the cellar after a brief melee in the dark. (Baby Alexa probably survives.) All soldiers regroup in the common room after hearing the disturbance.

- Sergeant Orth detains the Herzogs. He will question everyone else in the inn to determine their involvement. If he is satisfied that no one else is involved he will allow them to remain. Sergeant Orth and five of the soldiers will escort the Herzogs to the military camp; five more will remain behind.

- Once the Herzogs have been detained for questioning at the military camp, Sergeant Orth and his five men will return to the inn to guard it for the night and begin cataloguing the supplies.

- After questioning and deliberation, Griswold and Jarla will be executed as spies the following morning while Otto, Ilsa, and Gretchen will be given to some of the families in the camp follower train until they can be dropped at an orphanage along the way.

- Gabriela's fate is dependent on what the Referee thinks would be most interesting: she can be executed as one of the adults or press-ganged into the camp follower train as a loose end for the characters to later encounter.

- Assuming there are no other issues, the characters will be allowed to leave the following morning.

AFTERMATH

The Soldier's Rest is a tragedy in the making by the time the characters arrive, but it's hardly too late to change things. If you're an experienced Referee, you probably feel comfortable improvising to adjudicate the potential outcomes. If you don't or you're not used to this manner of scenario here are some probable outcomes:

The Characters Do Nothing
Why does everything revolve around them? They just want a good night's sleep. If they're staying in the inn, they get questioned and possibly detained if they have anything suspicious that they are unable to explain away. They are otherwise allowed to stay the rest of the night in the inn after the Steiners and the Herzogs are dealt with. The soldiers move them along the next day while trying to determine what to do with the place, which ultimately results in stripping everything of value and burning the place to the ground. Things proceed according to the above timeline.

The Characters Cast Spells
This escalates the situation depending on the sorts of spells being cast. A Catholic cleric spooks everyone into silence as the presence of an angry God seems all-too-real. The soldiers might be willing to rush an obvious adherent of Protestantism or some other religion; when in doubt, make a Morale check. Clerical magic might actually get people to stand down and de-escalate the situation depending upon the spell being cast.

Sorcery is an entirely different matter. There's nothing subtle about Magic-Users — all shouting and hand-waving with some bizarre effect at the end — unless you figure out some cover story for it. Most people will flee from an obvious Magic-User, although anyone passing a Morale check can choose to stay if they wish.

If the soldiers witness or hear of obvious Magic-User spells, their response is to retreat and return to the military camp. They will then mobilize as many soldiers as possible to surround the inn and burn it to the ground. This has the benefit of allowing the characters about twenty minutes to a half hour to flee, though the Herzogs are likely going to take the blame for it and be killed by the ensuing mob.

The Characters Flee with the Steiners During Dinner

This is probably the cleanest outcome. Griswold says soldiers are coming and asks the characters to keep quiet about the Steiners. The characters may offer to take the Steiners far away from here. Griswold offers them 50sp up front and says he'll give them the rest of any promised reward when they deliver proof the Steiners got to their destination. Assuming they keep their word, they're welcome to stay at *The Soldier's Rest* free of charge any time they're in the area. If they leave on friendly terms with the Herzogs, *The Soldier's Rest* would potentially make a fine stable investment as described on pages 53-54 of Rules & Magic. The characters and the Steiners camp out in the wilderness for the night and everyone is happy.

Take careful note of how much evidence they leave of their visit. If people were obviously here until very recently, Katharina Ruppel and her friends can track them (Anna Engel is a very skilled tracker). Their camp may be ambushed in the night by Katharina and her mercenaries. If she thinks she has time, she will no doubt get a squad of soldiers to back her up.

If the characters escort the Steiners to safety, it's probably nice if they hear that Lodwig Steiner is the butcher of Wendisch Rindorf somewhere along the way.

The Characters Turn in the Steiners

This is pretty simple: if the characters tell Katharina Ruppel about the Steiners, she will ride back to the military camp and summon the soldiers. They show up with two squads (two sergeants and twenty men total) to secure the inn. They will loudly announce their presence and give the Steiners hiding in the cellar ample time to surrender peacefully, "so none of the children get hurt." The Steiners and the Herzogs are taken into custody; the adults are executed and the children are placed with families until they can be dropped at an orphanage.

If the characters just tell the soldiers when they arrive, only one squad of soldiers comes to secure the inn but they still manage to avoid casualties by announcing themselves before entering rooms. The adults are executed but it's a lot less bloody.

In either case the characters can report to the military camp for their 200sp reward.

Waldemar is old enough to remember this night, though, and may come looking for revenge within the next five to ten years, or maybe he'll find a friendly ear in an orphanage who thinks the characters ought to pay for turning a poor family over to the authorities.

If Gabriela survives, she definitely seeks revenge. She may appear as the patron of a rival adventuring party sent to attack the characters, as the author of a Count of *Monte Cristo*-style revenge plot against them, or even as a 1st-level Specialist seeking her own revenge against them. She will be smart, though, and won't merely attack a superior force.

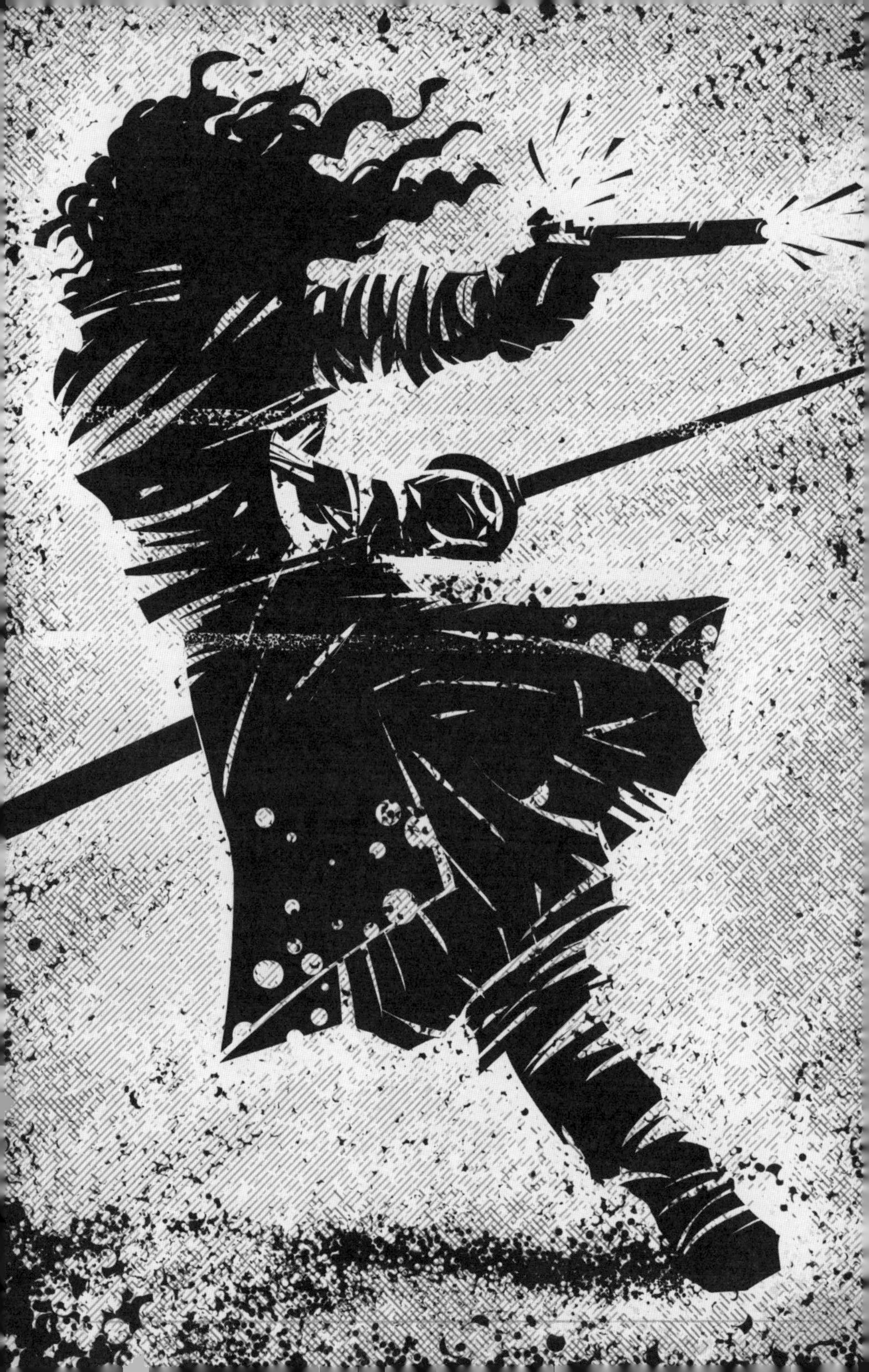

The Characters Attack the Spies
This is surprisingly effective: Katharina and Anna are ultimately disposable assets for the Imperial Army and their henchmen are just hired mercenaries. As long as nobody gets a good description of the people who did it, the characters can get away surprisingly clean.

Katharina and Anna will fight intelligently and will flee if the fight seems to go against them. The situation escalates if they can alert the soldiers; it takes one or two turns for armed squads to arrive at The Soldier's Rest from the camp. Remember that gunfire at the inn is audible from the military camp.

The Characters Attack the Soldiers
Hey, some will think they can win this. Unless they have a vastly superior force (in which case the soldiers are going to gather backup anyway), at least some of the soldiers will retreat, and if they alert the military camp the characters suddenly have a manhunt on their hands. Any surviving soldiers engaging the characters will report as much information as they can to their superiors; if they manage to evade capture long enough, they could end up being branded as enemies of the Emperor. Of course if they prove particularly adept at foiling or killing Imperial Army units, Protestant Union agents may approach them for recruitment…

The Characters Rob the Place
Maybe your characters are just sociopaths. In this case they might be able to get away clean as long as they don't kill anyone — the soldiers arrive and shockingly don't particularly believe this sob story about a robbery earlier in the evening. Everything proceeds as though the characters didn't intervene although Anna Engel might still track the characters to their camp just to figure out who they are. They might be attacked in the middle evening if their group seems particularly vulnerable, or if they match the descriptions of any bandits in the area.

Murders escalate the military response. The Imperial Army has a vested interest in stopping banditry in the area, and will respond swiftly if murdered bodies are found upon arriving at the inn. (Particularly since those bandits might be the very spies they seek.) The Army mobilizes a couple of squads, and Anna Engel can potentially track the characters back to their camp. Failure to find the characters' camp prompts the military to send horsemen in various directions to search the area. If the characters are found, these scouting parties may try to engage if they have the advantage, but will otherwise attempt to report the characters' location and mobilize more soldiers to apprehend or kill the characters.

Soldiers won't fight to the death — so engagements will likely have survivors who will report as much information as they can to their superiors, causing a manhunt like that described above.

Likewise, torching the inn will be visible from the military camp, and will draw soldiers to investigate and find the perpetrators.

THE INN

What started as Griswold Herzog's home funded by war profiteering money eventually grew into a trading post and later a full-blown inn, *The Soldier's Rest*. *The Soldier's Rest* is an ernhaus (a housebarn in traditional central German style) attached to a two-story inn. The inn looks newer than the farmhouse. A small series of fields to the north may hold grain, probably barley or rye if set in Bohemia; the state of growth depends on the current season. Assuming early spring, the grain is just starting to sprout.

The inn itself bears an iron sign hanging above the door proclaiming it "*The Soldier's Rest*." A stylized sleeping soldier, his hat lowered over his face to block the sun, is pictured on the sign. An old, twisted linden tree sits in the front yard.

With the exception of the front door of the inn the Herzogs keep most doors locked. During the daytime the pantry door, the door into the entryway, and the southern barn door are all routinely unlocked. At night only the front door of the inn is unlocked; those needing service can ring the bell on the counter or knock on the door between the common room and the entryway.

Griswold and Jarla both have key rings for the inn although Griswold gives out his copies of the room keys to patrons. Jarla has the master set.

THE OLD LINDEN TREE

A hollow near the top of the tree is the dead drop location used by Protestant Union intelligencers. It is lined with oiled canvas and contains a wooden box to prevent rain water from damaging missives. If the characters climb and search the tree (the hollow isn't visible from the ground) they will find an encrypted message within. It can be decrypted with the appropriate key (not available here), a few hours' work and a Languages check at -2, the *Comprehend Languages* spell, or any other reasonable ploy the characters develop.

The encoded message probably relates to Catholic League troop movements although it may also contain campaign-relevant information of the Referee's devising.

Interested parties may be willing to pay 150sp for the intelligence contained therein, although exceedingly well-placed operatives and government officials may be willing to pay more. It is up to the Referee whether the Imperial Army or other officials would be willing to pay for such intelligence or whether they would execute the characters on principle.

COMMON ROOM
Many of the NPCs in this scenario are present in the common room when the characters arrive. Jarla and Gabriela help serve patrons and take care of little Gretchen. Otto and Ilsa are playing and potentially underfoot.

Griswold keeps a sword and an old matchlock arquebus behind the bar just in case things get out of hand. They accompany him to bed when he locks the house at night.

Tables comfortably seat eight so there are plenty of empty seats.

Lodwig, Wilhelmina, Waldemar, Konrad, Dieter, and Alexa are eating at the table on the far right of the room, closest to the fireplace, when the characters enter.

THE INN & TRADING POST
When the characters arrive, there are four rooms available as well as stabling enough for two horses.

SERVICE	PRICE
Inn Room	2sp
Stabling	1sp
Meal (stew)	3cp
Drink (lager)	1cp

The Herzogs are likely to have most standard goods on hand as listed in Rules & Magic, pages 29-30. Assume rural prices for all available goods. They only have 10 iron rations on hand, and they are only willing to sell 50 standard rations. They can be persuaded to sell more standard rations if the characters offer an exorbitant price like 5sp per ration. The Herzogs will absolutely not sell their last 50 standard rations.

If an item seems particularly exotic, then they either don't have it or you can assume a flat 1-in-6 chance that it's available. If you're generous or it seems more likely to be in stock, assume 2-in-6.

ENTRYWAY
A hallway. Doors lead to the barn, common room, kitchen, and sitting room. There is no door between the entryway and the kitchen.

PANTRY
This area gets used for storage of any dry goods as well as food to be prepared as part of the day's meals. An incline leads down to the root cellar.

Many items for sale are currently stored here; the standard rations are down in the cellar.

CELLAR
The equivalent of 1d6 × 100 days' worth of standard rations are stored down here where the cool temperatures will prevent spoilage. Any remaining items for sale that won't fit in the pantry are stored here.

The Steiners' gear is stored here, which includes saddlebags, two backpacks, a couple of sets of common clothes and winter clothes, three bedrolls, a lantern, two flasks of oil, five waterskins, seventy days' iron rations, and 28sp in assorted jewelry and coin. As noted in their statistics they also have two flintlock arquebuses, two powder horns, two shot bags, a sword, and a knife.

If this area is investigated after dark, the Steiners will be here: Lodwig, Wilhelmina, Waldemar (age 8), Konrad (age 5), Dieter (age 2), and Alexa (newborn).

Anyone searching this area will note a patch of disturbed earth in the northeastern corner of the room. Digging will reveal a locked strongbox (the key is on Griswold's key ring). The strongbox contains 500sp and a strange idol of a leering devil Griswold found in an abandoned village while on campaign. He kept it as a memento and it is potentially worth 200sp to the right buyer. It is up to the Referee whether it has more significance than just a strange memento. If it holds any magic, Griswold certainly doesn't know about it. If Jarla knew he still had it, she would probably make him get rid of it. The devil idol likely has no strange abilities, although a devious Referee may determine it is enchanted with a *Magic Aura*. The Referee may change the idol to another item connected to any conspiracy or strange event in his campaign; it has no significance beyond being yet another loose end to investigate if the characters go searching.

SITTING ROOM
This plain room contains a table, some chairs, and a Bible. A crucifix hangs upon the wall.

MASTER BEDROOM
A couple of beds and a chest of drawers dominate this room. In addition to several sets of common clothes in various sizes, 165sp is hidden in the bottom of the drawers.

In the wintertime the Herzogs often sleep with the door to this room open so as to better receive heat from the kitchen.

KITCHEN
A wood stove for a cooking fire sits against the northeastern wall. No matter the season the fire is usually burning during the day although it will sit unused at night during the warmer months.

BARN
Goats and a lone cow inhabit the pens along the western wall while stables for horses dominate the eastern wall. The Herzogs keep a single horse. The Steiners' horse is also stabled here; the Herzogs will claim it is theirs if asked. A cart and several farm tools round out this crowded space.

INN ROOMS
These rooms each contain a bed and a dresser. They may contain additional items depending upon the occupants therein.

THE MILITARY CAMP

Captain Morgan Carne is a "Walsman," specifically a Catholic exile from Wales, and was pleased enough to find a place in the Catholic south of the Holy Roman Empire. (If it becomes relevant, he speaks English, German, and Welsh.) In the process of leading his soldiers back to Wallenstein's main force to the southwest, the Imperial Army camp is about a quarter mile up the road from *The Soldier's Rest*. If the characters decide to investigate, the camp comprises a series of tents in formation with the officers' tents and supply tents in the middle. Among the forces stationed here are Captain Carne, 13 sergeants, and 128 privates, subtracting any that might be at *The Soldier's Rest*, of course. There are roughly twice as many camp followers, making the camp about 450 people in total. It contains 10gp, 890sp, and 1600cp divided among all tents in the camp and 5400 rations found among the cook tents, with a few found among the camp followers. Lest your players need to be reminded: standing between the characters and all the loot and equipment are 142 trained soldiers and twice as many camp followers, so good luck with that.

Don't forget: gunfire at *The Soldier's Rest* is audible from camp so any particularly loud combats will draw army investigators. It takes about one turn for a ready squad to reach *The Soldier's Rest* or about two turns for a squad to get ready and approach the inn.

Captain Carne: Armor 17, Move 90', 2nd Level Fighter, 9hp, pistol 1d8 (1d4 mêlée) or sword 1d8, Morale 10. Pikeman's armor, buff coat, morion, tassets, longsword, flintlock pistol, powder horn, shot bag, 21sp.

Sergeant: Armor 16, Move 90', 1st Level Fighter, 5hp, arquebus 1d8 (1d6 mêlée) or sword 1d8, Morale 9. Pikeman's armor, buff coat, morion, longsword, flintlock arquebus, powder horn, shot bag.

Privates: Armor 14, Move 120', 0-Level, 4hp, pike 1d10 or sword 1d8, Morale 8. Buff coat, morion, longsword, pike.

Camp Follower: Armor 12, Move 120', 0-Level, 3hp, punch 1d2 or dagger 1d4, Morale 7.

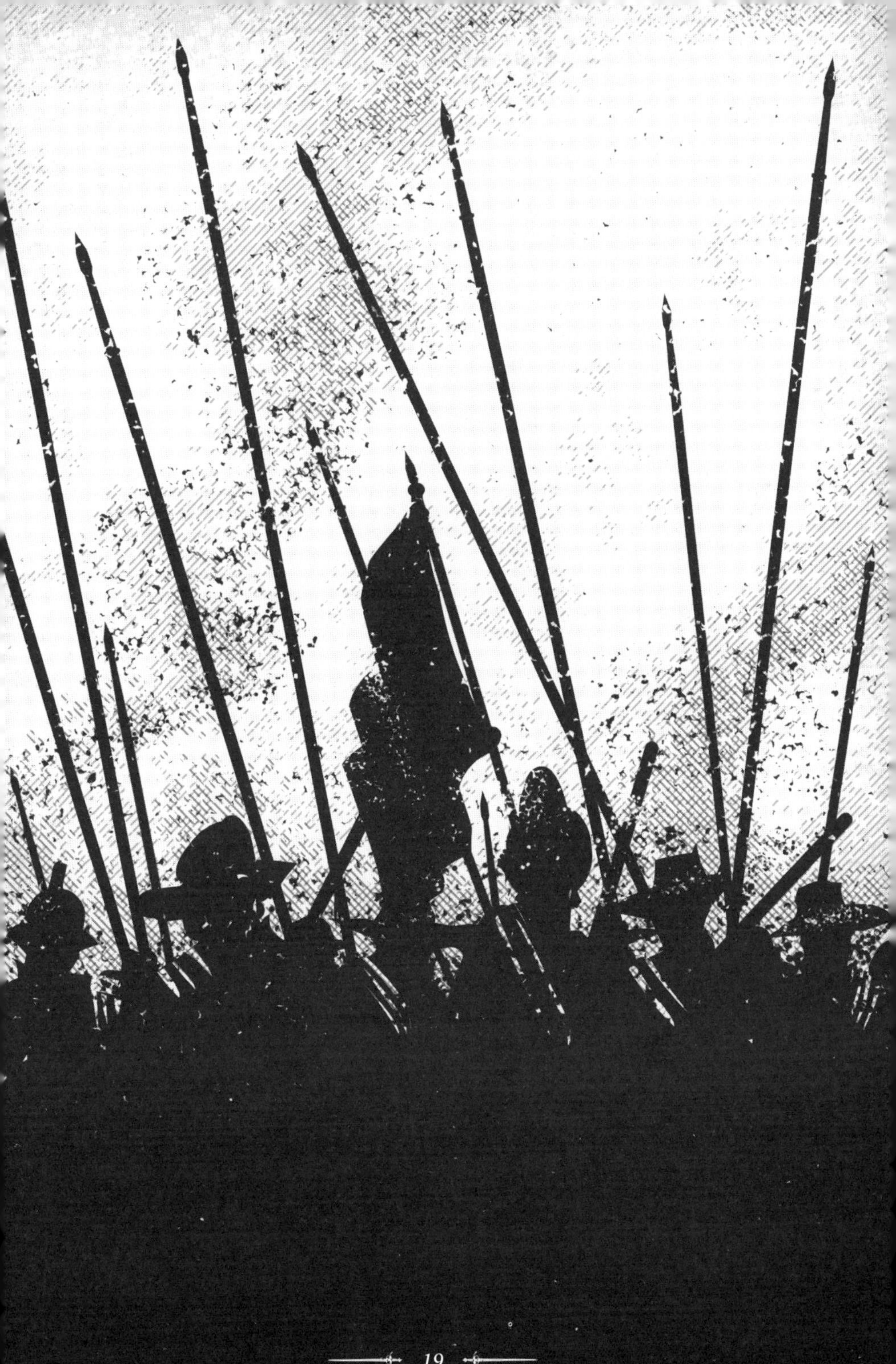

DRAMATIS PERSONAE

The write-ups that follow give a bit of background, description, and roleplaying hints. The characters are unlikely to fully interact with everyone listed here, so only focus on those that interest your players and let the rest fade into the background.

GRISWOLD HERZOG, INNKEEPER

Griswold fought in the war for the Imperial Army and retired a bitter man. The Sack of Magdeburg killed whatever remaining enthusiasm he had for the Catholic cause; he's tired of the war he and wants to see it end. He's been operating *The Soldier's Rest* as a dead drop location for Protestant intelligencers for the past eight months.

This would be dangerous enough but he happened to take in a group of refugees just as the Imperial Army passed through en route to rejoin Wallenstein's army. Not wanting to draw undue attention, he's been hiding these refugees in his inn.

Griswold is average height but broad in build; he's the sort of guy to project "bigness" when you look at him even though he's not particularly large. His left ear is notched and scarred, and he has a horizontal scar below the orbit of his left eye where a musket ball bounced off his left cheekbone and punched through his ear.

Griswold is tired. Despite his size he projects a world-weary Harry Dean Stanton exterior. Sigh a lot when you play him, particularly when he stands or sits.

Griswold Herzog: Armor 12, Move 120', 1st Level Fighter, 7hp, arquebus 1d8 (1d6 mêlée) or sword 1d8, Morale 9.

JARLA HERZOG, INNKEEPER

Jarla married Griswold before he went off to war and they had two children, Gabriela and Ulrich. Ulrich took ill while they were on the road and died when he was an infant. She and Gabriela were camp followers while Griswold was on campaign. She saw enough horror out there to agree with Griswold's assessment that the war serves no God in Heaven and supports his decision to lend what aid he can to the Protestant Union's cause. She is frightened at the prospect of the Imperial Army learning of his activities. She sleeps poorly these days and largely busies herself with work. Since the Steiners have arrived at *The Soldier's Rest* she has barely slept.

Jarla bears cheeks lightly marked by a pox that afflicted her when she was much younger, and usually keeps her straw-colored hair under a bonnet while working. She isn't quite unhealthily thin but is definitely thin enough to draw remarks, and the dark circles under her eyes speak of late nights.

Jarla barely speaks when travelers are about, worried as she is about drawing attention to the Steiners. She largely talks to be polite and seems a bit nervous when she does; she attends to Gretchen when others are about which is a shame, really; if the characters return when she is in better spirits she's definitely the cleverer of the pair — always quick with a joke — and has a lovely singing voice.

Jarla Herzog: Armor 12, Move 120', 0-Level, 3hp, dagger 1d4, Morale 7.

DER SOLDAT RUFT

GABRIELA HERZOG, STABLE GIRL

Gabriela is the exact sort of girl who daydreams about life beyond her little village. Only sixteen, she doesn't remember life before the war, though she was old enough when her brother Ulrich was born to remember his death. Since the family settled at *The Soldier's Rest*, Gabriela has been in charge of the stables. She also helps in the inn when her mother looks after the little ones.

If the characters are full of tales of far-off lands, Gabriela is the one likely to listen in rapt attention if her duties allow. She's also the sort to run away as a hireling if the characters try to work that angle, although that would break her parents' hearts.

Gabriela is plain and still a little awkward, but she's wiry from doing chores and working with animals. She has her mother's straw-colored hair, although it's usually a mess, and she rarely bothers to wear a bonnet.

Gabriela is every wide-eyed teenager with charming earnestness and dreams of the big city. She likes to collect stories from all the travelers who pass through the inn.

Gabriela Herzog: Armor 12, Move 120', 0-Level, 3hp, dagger 1d4, Morale 7.

THE YOUNGER HERZOGS

As previously noted, Ulrich would have been fourteen this year had he lived. The others are Otto (age 4), Ilsa (age 2), and Gretchen (newborn). The toddlers will try to run if there's trouble and only have 1hp. How you play Otto and Ilsa is up to you: they can be cute or comic relief. If you want to set a creepier mood, play them like the twins from *The VVitch*.

LODWIG STEINER, DESERTER

Months of campaigning convinced Lodwig of the futile nature of this war. He was convinced he was a Catholic soldier to be fed into the waiting maw of the Lion of the North with his family left behind to be ravaged by Swedish soldiers.

He convinced a handful of soldiers of the same, and they all agreed to take their families and any equipment they could carry and flee. When they made camp near the village of Wendisch Rindorf they executed their plan. They loaded horses with supplies, burned the nearby village so that the Imperial Army camp would be unable to use it to resupply, and fled in separate directions so they would be harder to capture.

In his heart he knows that there are villagers who probably didn't escape and people who starved for lack of food, but he had to protect his own family. He's having a hard time reconciling it, but that's something he can worry about later when he's safely away from the front.

He bought his way north with supplies and military intelligence. One of these intelligence contacts recommended Lodwig pass by *The Soldier's Rest* on his way northwest, as Griswold Herzog is apparently known among the right kind of people to be friendly with all manner of dissidents and enemy agents.

Lodwig isn't quite thirty, but bears the scars of war and has the greying beard and sunken eyes of a much older man. He dresses plainly, attempting to avoid drawing attention to himself.

Lodwig Steiner: Armor 12, Move 120', 1st Level Fighter, 6hp, arquebus 1d8 (1d6 mêlée) or sword 1d8, Morale 9.

WILHELMINA STEINER, REFUGEE

Wilhelmina is tired beyond tired — tired of marching, tired of running, tired of the war, tired of too many Gods. Isn't there just the One? Why the division, then?

Perhaps more than being tired, Wilhelmina is angry. She knows it's a long road to somewhere safe, either in the northwest or in a foreign kingdom somewhere. They'll have to skirt around the front lines to head to freedom, and she'll gladly fight any soldier she comes across so that her children might have a future.

Wilhelmina is small and unassuming until you see her vibrant eyes peering out from those black circles. She speaks like a good, dutiful wife, but there's a fire in her that she can only barely contain. She's pleasant if people are pleasant, but if they seem the least bit aggressive she almost dares them to try something.

Wilhelmina Steiner: Armor 12, Move 120', 0-Level, 5hp, arquebus 1d8 (1d6 mêlée) or dagger 1d4, Morale 9.

THE YOUNGER STEINERS

The Steiner children are Waldemar (age 8), Konrad (age 5), Dieter (age 2), and Alexa (newborn). Waldemar has 2hp while the others each have 1hp. All are likely to run if there's trouble.

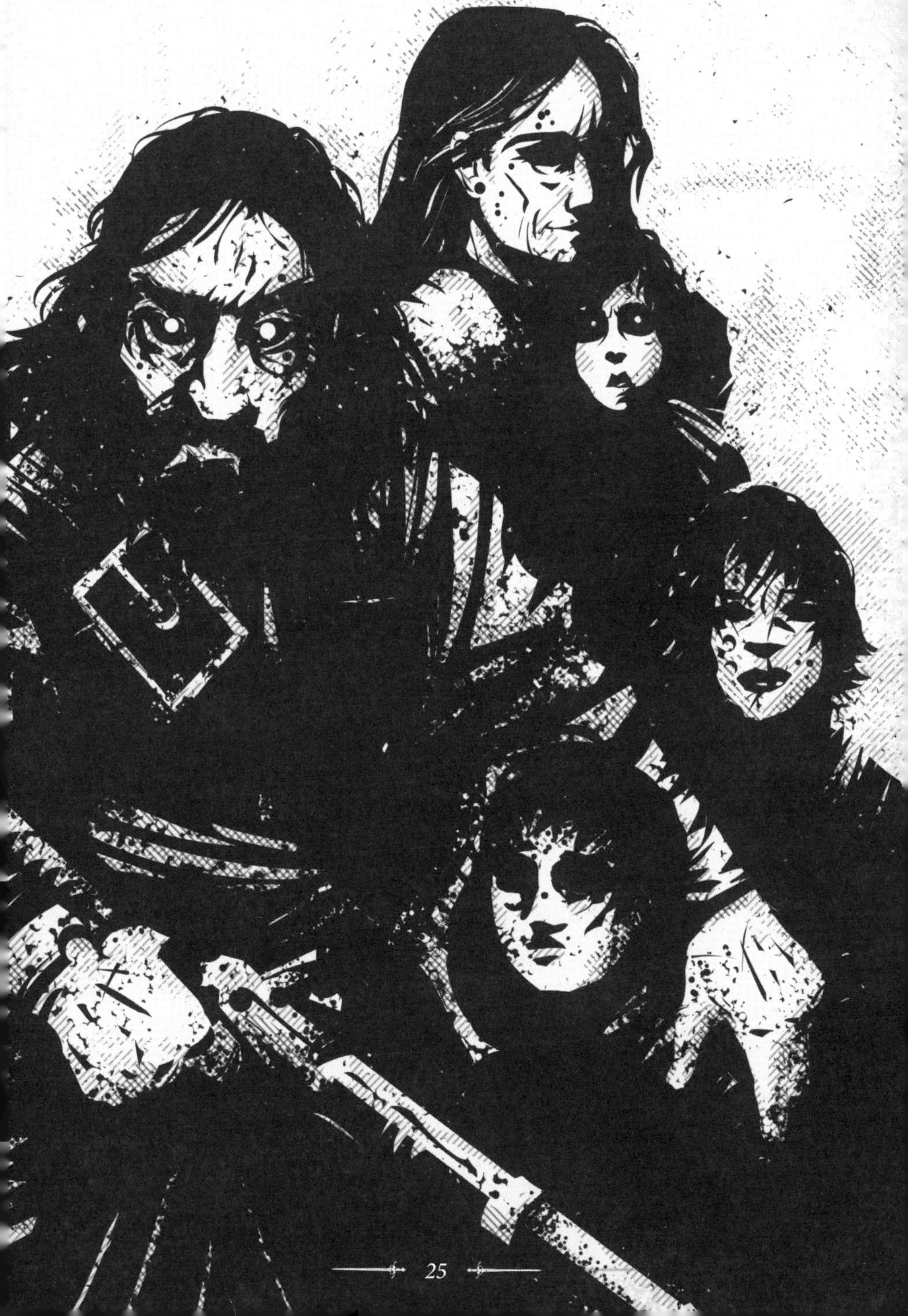

SERGEANT JOHANN ORTH

Sergeant Orth is a good Catholic in the midst of a bloodbath and he hasn't adjusted terribly well. He's not about to desert the cause — God abhors a coward — but he's not sure this is what the churches wanted. More importantly, his enthusiasm for the cause is waning under the overwhelming evidence that he's living on borrowed time. When his company received the orders to return to the front, he knew that would eventually involve facing down Gustavus Adolphus, the Lion of the North. The man has never lost a battle so that likely means Orth will be dead inside a year.

Tomorrow Captain Carne's company continues to head southwest to reconvene with Wallenstein's forces. Captain Carne has received intelligence that foreign spies and saboteurs may be active in the area and is dispatching Sergeant Orth to search it in the middle of the night. Orth plans on discharging his duty — he would hate to think that lives were lost because he let a spy go free — but he has lost his taste for the bloodshed of his countrymen. If someone met him earnestly and asked him to, perhaps, overlook something suspicious he might let it slide just to give someone a chance of surviving this madness.

Sergeant Orth is tall and slim with crooked teeth and dark complexion. He wears a leather patch over his right eye and a wedding band for a woman long dead.

Sergeant Orth: Armor 16, Move 90', 1st Level Fighter, 5hp, arquebus 1d8 (1d6 mêlée) or sword 1d8, Morale 9. Pikeman's armor, buff coat, morion, longsword, flintlock arquebus, powder horn, shot bag, 11sp.

Privates (10): Armor 14, Move 120', 0-Level, 4hp, sword 1d8, Morale 8. Buff coat, morion, longsword.

KATHARINA RUPPEL, IMPERIAL INTELLIGENCER

Widowed like so many during this war, Katharina made a living as a traveling adventurer, moving around Europe as a scholar and occasional pickpocket. She was eventually recruited as an intelligence asset by the Imperial Army. Working for the Empire certainly beats picking pockets and robbing tombs.

Katharina has evidence that intelligence operatives for the Protestant Union are operating in the vicinity of *The Soldier's Rest*, although they may be a few days in any direction. She has warned Captain Carne of this information and is watching carefully for any irregularities that she may interrogate further. Unlike Carne, she has few compunctions about ruining someone's life or killing; she's a dedicated agent and the work she does for the Emperor gives her meaning. If she suspects the characters are involved in espionage and questioning them seems too difficult, she may just kill them if she thinks she can get away with it.

For her cover she claims to be married to Jakob.

If the intelligencers' room or camp is accessed and searched they have: four backpacks, four bedrolls, four waterskins, two saddlebags, a set of cooking pots, a spyglass, a grappling hook, two crowbars, two lanterns, six flasks of lamp oil, ten torches, ten iron spikes, a mallet, twenty feet of chain, four coils of 50' ropes, and a total of 120 days' iron rations. There is also a relatively complete map of the area.

Katharina has fair skin, dark hair, pockmarked cheeks, and a broad-brimmed hat. She's the most personable of the lot and the most likely to speak with the characters. She's easy with a smile or a laugh although her smile can become a trifle predatory if she is trying to get at information with which the characters are reluctant to part.

Katharina Ruppel: Armor 14, Move 120', 3rd Level Specialist, 13hp, pistol 1d8 (1d4 mêlée) or rapier 1d8, Morale 10. Charisma 14, Dexterity 13. Languages 3, Sleight of Hand 4, Stealth 4. Buff coat, 2 pistols, rapier, powder horn, shot bag. 2gp, 75sp.

ANNA ENGEL, IMPERIAL INTELLIGENCER

When the Imperial war machine needed scouts, someone must have told them the weirdo in the woods knew her way around the wilderness.

Anna's lived in the woods her whole life, and while she would have been content to keep to herself she can hardly complain about the pay. Besides, whenever she's tired of it she can always leave. What are they going to do, track her? If Katharina has someone she needs to find or if they need to head into the wilderness for a few days, Anna is the one to ensure they find whatever target they seek. She's not nearly as assertive or verbose as Katharina but if you're suspicious enough she'll be the one to track you down in the night and hold a gun to your head.

Anna claims to be married to Michael as part of her cover. She is willowy, fair-haired (which she wears short), and fair-skinned. She looks the best-rested of anyone in the tavern and is generally taciturn. Anna keeps her silver in her pouch but her gold in her shoe.

Anna Engel: Armor 15, Move 120', 2nd Level Specialist, 10hp, pistol 1d8 (1d4 mêlée) or rapier 1d8, Morale 10. Dexterity 16. Bushcraft 4, Stealth 4. Buff coat, 2 pistols, rapier, powder horn, shot bag. 1gp, 70sp.

THE MERCENARIES

Jakob Deines and Michael Kniess accompany Katharina Ruppel and Anna Engel and are well-compensated for their bodyguarding duties. The mercenaries keep their silver in their pouches and their gold in their shoes. Jakob and Michael are both rough-hewn men with scars, clearly familiar with violence, a Rosencrantz and Guildenstern of thuggery.

Mercenaries: Armor 13, Move 120', 1st Level Fighter, 6hp, sword 1d8, Morale 9. Buff coat, longsword, 1gp, 37sp.

CELLAR MOUND

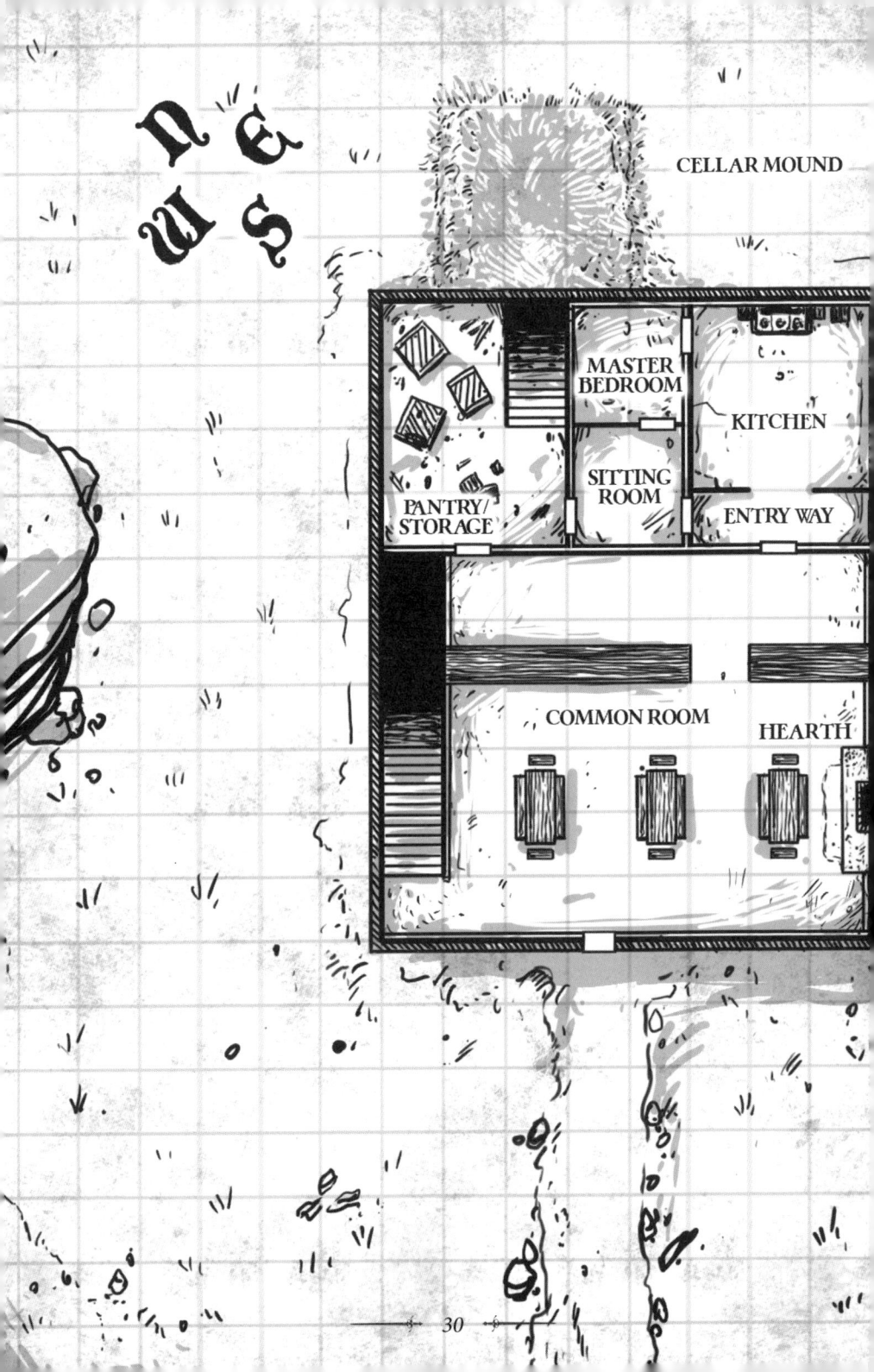

MASTER BEDROOM

KITCHEN

SITTING ROOM

PANTRY/ STORAGE

ENTRY WAY

COMMON ROOM

HEARTH

THE INN
GROUND FLOOR

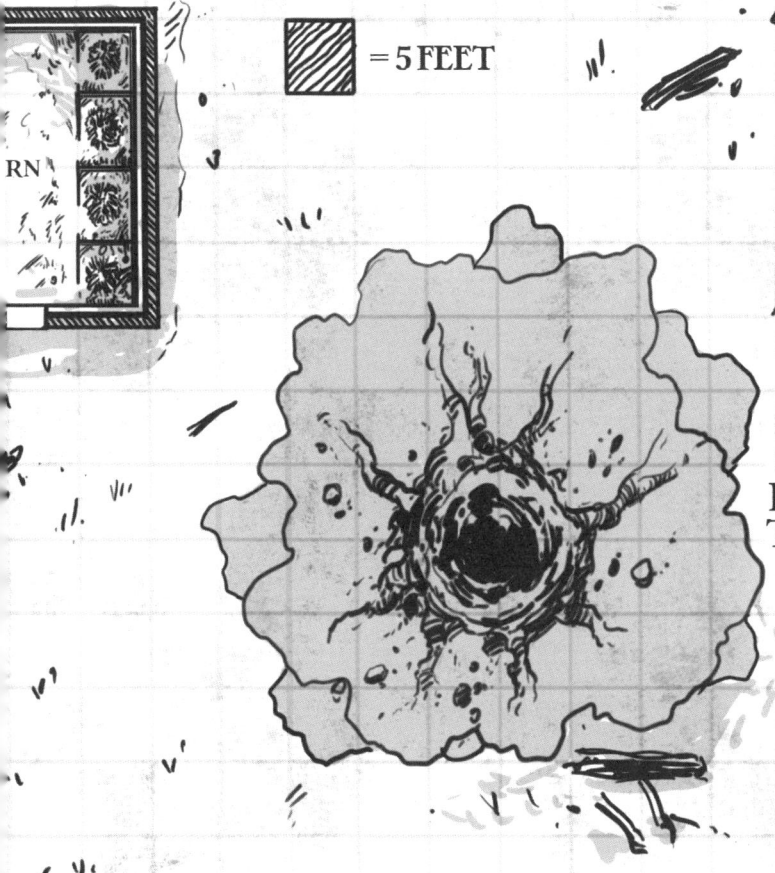

▨ = 5 FEET

OLD
LIME
TREE

THE INN
SECOND FLOOR / CELLAR

INN ROOMS

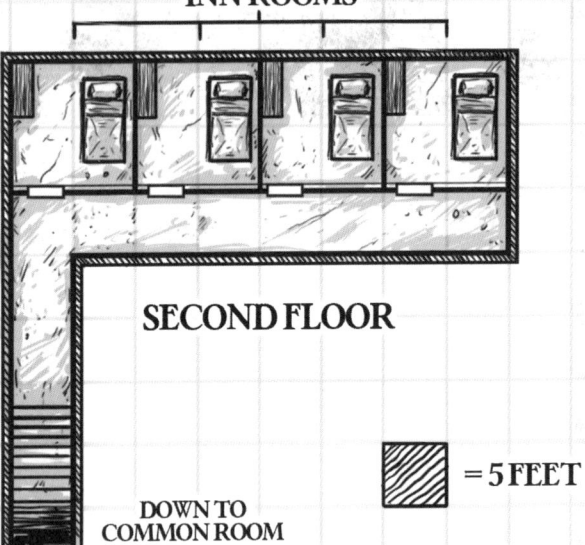

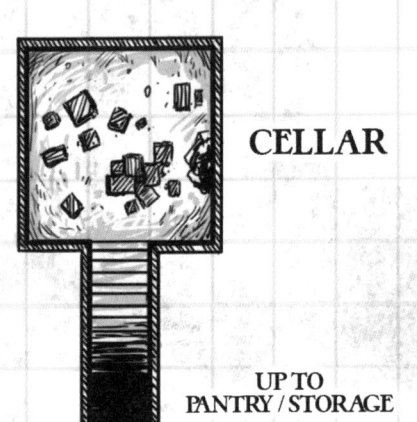

SECOND FLOOR

DOWN TO COMMON ROOM

☐ = 5 FEET

CELLAR

UP TO PANTRY / STORAGE